ART IS IN
THE COOKBOOK

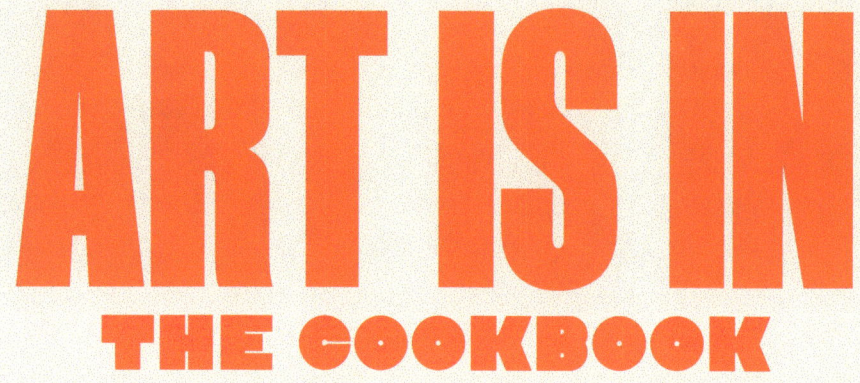

ART IS IN
THE COOKBOOK

By Chef Kevin Mathieson
with Shawna Wagman

Book Compilation by Stephanie Mathieson

Editing by Kerry-Lee Smith and Marguerite Monnin

In Loving Memory by Chef François Payard, friends and family

Recipe Testing by Jose Armando Diaz, Sasha Nicholas and Alexandra Hanssens

---

PHOTOGRAPHY BY NICOLAI GREGORY WITH CONTRIBUTIONS BY ASHLEY FRASER
ART DIRECTION & BOOK DESIGN BY CHELSEA NELSON

INTRODUCTION

A Book Warmly Shaped by Time 12
The Bakery 16
The Cookbook 26

THE ART OF BREAD

The Autolyse Method 30
The Best Home-Baked Loaves 32

Dynamite Breads

Poolish (Dynamite Starter) 34
Dynamite White Bread 36
Rosemary Garlic 36
Cheddar Jalapeno 36
Kalamata Olive 36
English Muffins 38

Sourdoughs

Mother (Sourdough Starter) 40
Kevin's White Sourdough 42
Herb & Cheese 47
Rosemary & Garlic 48
Whole Wheat & Rye 50
Raisin Bread 51
Pizza Dough Ball 120

Specialty Breads

Buttermilk Multiseed Bread 52
Crazy Grain Bread 56
Potato Buns 58
Holiday Bread 60
Hot Cross Buns 62
Brioche Pullman Bread 64

ENTS

THE ART OF BRUNCH

Croque Monsieur / Madame 68
Bechamel Sauce 69
Hollandaise Sauce 70
Eggs Benny 74
Maple Fennel Sausage 72
Buttermilk Pancakes 73
French Toast Stack 76
Candied Bacon 77
Quiche Lorraine 78
Loaded Breakfast Sandwich 80

THE ART OF LUNCH

Art Is In House Mayo 84
Chicken Caesar Sandwich 86
Buttermilk Brined Roast Chicken 88
Caesar Mayo 88
Crispy Pickle Melt Sandwich 90
Spicy Mayo 92
Caramelized Onions 92
Fried Pickle Spice Blend 92
Thai Curry Chicken Sandwich 94
Thai Curry Roasted Chicken Breast 94
Thai Curry Mayo 94
Butternut Squash Caponata Sandwich 96
Squash Caponata Mix 96
House Vinaigrette 96
Lemon Chive Mayo 97
Pistachio Pesto 97
Grilled Cheese 98
Art Is In House Ketchup 100
Kevin's Clam Chowder 102
Kevin's Vegan Thai Curry Soup 104
Caesar Salad & Dressing 105
Maple Pork Tourtière with Roasted Squash 106
Beef Brisket Poutine Tourtière 108
Kevin's Meatballs 110
Gnocchi & Technique 112
Nonna Sauce 114
Mac & Cheese Sauce 116

THE ART OF PIZZA

Pizza Dough Shaping 120
Pizza Making Technique 122
Kevin's Pizza Sauce 124
Parmesan Dip 126

Pizzas

Cheese Louise 127
Hipster Pepperoni 128
Tarte Flambée 130
Kevin's Hot Honey 130
Spaghetti with a Chance of Meatballs 132
Vermont Veggie 134
Lost in Wakefield 135

THE ART OF PASTRY

Chewy Chocolate Walnut Cookies 138
Peanut Butter Cookies 140
Financiers 141
Spicy Molasses Cookies 142
Macarons 144
White Chocolate Filling 150
Chocolat Crémeux 151
Chocolate Espresso Brownies 148
Chocolate Ganache Topping 149
Butter Croissants 154
Croissant Folding Technique 158
Chocolate Croissants 156
Raspberry Scones 160
Cheddar & Chive Scones 162
Pâte Sucrée (Tart Shells) 163
Lemon Tarts 164
Banana Tarts 165
Old-Fashioned Potato Buttermilk Doughnuts with Maple Glaze 168
Berliners 170
Raspberry Jam 172
Vanilla Pastry Cream 173
Cream Topping 166
Art Is In Hot Chocolate 167
Canelés de Bordeaux 174
Pâte Brisée (Pie Dough) 176
Puff Pastry 178
Galette des Rois 180

IN LOVING MEMORY

Letters from Family & Friends 186

A BOOK WARMLY SHAPED BY TIME

By Shawna Wagman

When Kevin's text message arrived, it was already a done deal, "There's no one I'd rather write this book with than you," he wrote. Back then, I was a food writer for the city magazine and I had interviewed Kevin for several articles. The idea that we'd be writing this cookbook together one day had become a refrain. "When are we going to write the book?" he'd say. "Let's do it," I'd say. There were fits and starts. Kevin started adapting his recipes for home cooks and soon a literary agent expressed interest in getting the book published. But life kept getting in the way; months and years passed. Kevin had long been battling a serious illness when the pandemic hit, and I was in the midst of a career transition. That text message signaled the moment we agreed to start writing the book in earnest.

True to his spirit of generosity, Kevin was determined to share with the world his hard-won kitchen secrets, his tried-and-tested techniques and his passion for food made simply from scratch. Kevin tragically passed away in 2023 before the project was complete. This book in your hands is his dream come true, a genuine labour of love shared with Stephanie, his partner in life and in the bakery. While processing unimaginable grief, Stephanie found tremendous joy in bringing the Art Is In cookbook to fruition. She assembled recipe testers and editors and lovingly found ways to add snippets of notes Kevin wrote and left around the house.

In the early days of conceptualizing this book, Kevin and I met up in bookstores to dissect our favourite cookbooks, flipping through them and making notes about what his book could be.

CANELÉS, PAGE 174

Next we started to meet at the bakery and he'd tell me stories about growing up in Winnipeg and working as a cook at the Fort Garry Hotel. He'd surprised himself by winning a local pastry competition and said it was what set him off on this path. While gently folding dough and stretching pizzas, he'd talk to me about what it was like to work at some of the best bakeries in the world, like Ladurée and Fauchon in Paris. He'd bring me things to taste and then humbly accept my rave reviews with the same understated response: "Aw, thanks. I'm so glad you like it."

I still remember the first time I tasted Art Is In bread at the stall of an outdoor farmers market. I was carrying my then newborn daughter and stopped to pick up a sample of a baguette. This was no ordinary bread. The complexity of its flavour and texture was unlike anything I'd tasted before. When I met the baker a few days later, I had so many questions but my weary postpartum brain struggled to keep up with his animated explanation of the two-day-long baking process: the feeding of the sourdough starter, the constant attention and gentle folding of the dough, the shaping of it by hand. It all started to sound a lot like taking care of a baby. And, come to think of it, a lot like writing a cookbook.

Not only did I get a crash course in artisanal baking but it was the start of a special friendship. We had a food-centric bond, the kind where I'd deliver full reports with photos to Kevin of everything I'd eaten in Paris, and he'd send me text messages that would say things like "You should come try our tourtière ravioli with caramelized chicken velouté on our garlic toast."

As my daughter grew, so did Kevin's bakery (and his family) and we began to celebrate each other's milestones with shared birthday cakes and bakery anniversaries. Over our 17 years of friendship, there were babies born, business dinners, bat mitzvah brunches and funerals — all occasions where we could count on Kevin's food to comfort, nourish and delight. Meanwhile, I was lucky enough to have a permanent backstage pass (with tasting privileges) as Kevin proudly grew his business alongside Stephanie. Together they realized Kevin's vision for Art Is In Bakery, a one-of-a-kind destination: my favourite place in the world to eat.

Lucky for all of us, Kevin landed in Ottawa as a young man to work in restaurants. It's where he met his true love and made the easy decision to stay and build a beautiful family and a bakery. He continued to travel widely to visit professional kitchens around the world— from hole-in-the-walls to Michelin-starred meals. He was always learning and researching—always finding new ways to coax the most deliciousness out of even the simplest ingredients. He lived his life this way too, which is one of the things I admired most about him. And I'm thrilled that spirit is alive in this book, forever. As Kevin would say: I hope you like it.

THE BAKERY

Let's start with a bit of the backstory, years before Art Is In Bakery was named the #1 place to eat in Ottawa...

I'm a young pastry chef working at a fine dining restaurant in Quebec, just across the river from Parliament Hill. I tell my new boss that instead of using frozen wholesale baguettes I want to make fresh homemade bread—like the sourdough loaves I love in Brooklyn and Paris that are slow fermented, tender-chewy inside and impossibly crunchy outside, radiating a lingering tang. This is around the time that the artisan food movement is hitting big cities across North America and I am determined to get more people on board. Nobody in our sleepy government town was baking anything like it at the time.

I'm classically trained in French pastry—I've worked like a dog to learn how to make the perfect butter croissant, absorbing centuries-old secrets from some of the best chefs in the world, but it's the rustic loaves of slow-fermented bread that are taking over my life.

I love how mysterious and playful dough can be—how small variation in temperature or humidity can radically impact its character. My mood, too, seems to be a key ingredient (but more on that later).

So, I start experimenting with my own recipes, aiming for something I can produce efficiently for the restaurant's daily demands. I perfect my *poolish* (a yeast, water and flour mixture) which pre-ferments for 14 hours before the bread dough is even mixed. I get an elastic dough, with a texture somewhere between fresh hand-pulled mozzarella and marshmallow fluff. Sure, the preparation is long—nearly three days—but the work is minimal, just a little bit of mixing and a lot of patience.

CHEF KEVIN MATHIESON

The dough is beautiful, and it makes me so happy: it's yeasty and fruity, like mild banana mixed with pineapple. I know that my culinary mentors—most of them bread traditionalists—would never approve of this crazy bubbly concoction, but I want to make what I love. When I touch the wobbly mass, the dough responds. The bread is alive, and so am I! I form long rustic loaves and slather the tops with olive oil and a shower of kosher salt (because crystal size matters, but I'll talk about salt use later). When it hits the heat of the oven the dough blows up—big air pockets cracking beneath a dark burnished crust. The aroma is incredible and when I taste it, the flavours explode. **It's Dynamite!**

The name "Dynamite" stuck.

Eighteen years later and my Dynamite bread is still one of the most popular menu items at Art Is In Bakery. The word dynamite has become a bit of a thing. It's the word for the feeling I get in my gut when the dough is just right. It's the excitement of inventing a new sandwich special (like the Philly cheese steak on a pretzel bun with buffalo mozzarella and a red wine veal demi-glace). Dynamite is what fuels me through exhaustion and solitary nights spent between stacks of bins of fermenting dough. It's the word that comes to mind when I'm serving brunch for 1000 people, with when the line up to buy my breads and baked goods is the longest one at local farmers markets. It's the sense of independence and love my baking brings me, the delight of building my dream bakery inside a 3,500 square-foot industrial warehouse in a wonky off-the-beaten-path location bordering two provinces—and watching it, by word-of-mouth, become one of the top food destinations in the Canadian capital.

"Dynamite is what fuels me through exhaustion and solitary nights spent between stacks of bins of fermenting dough.

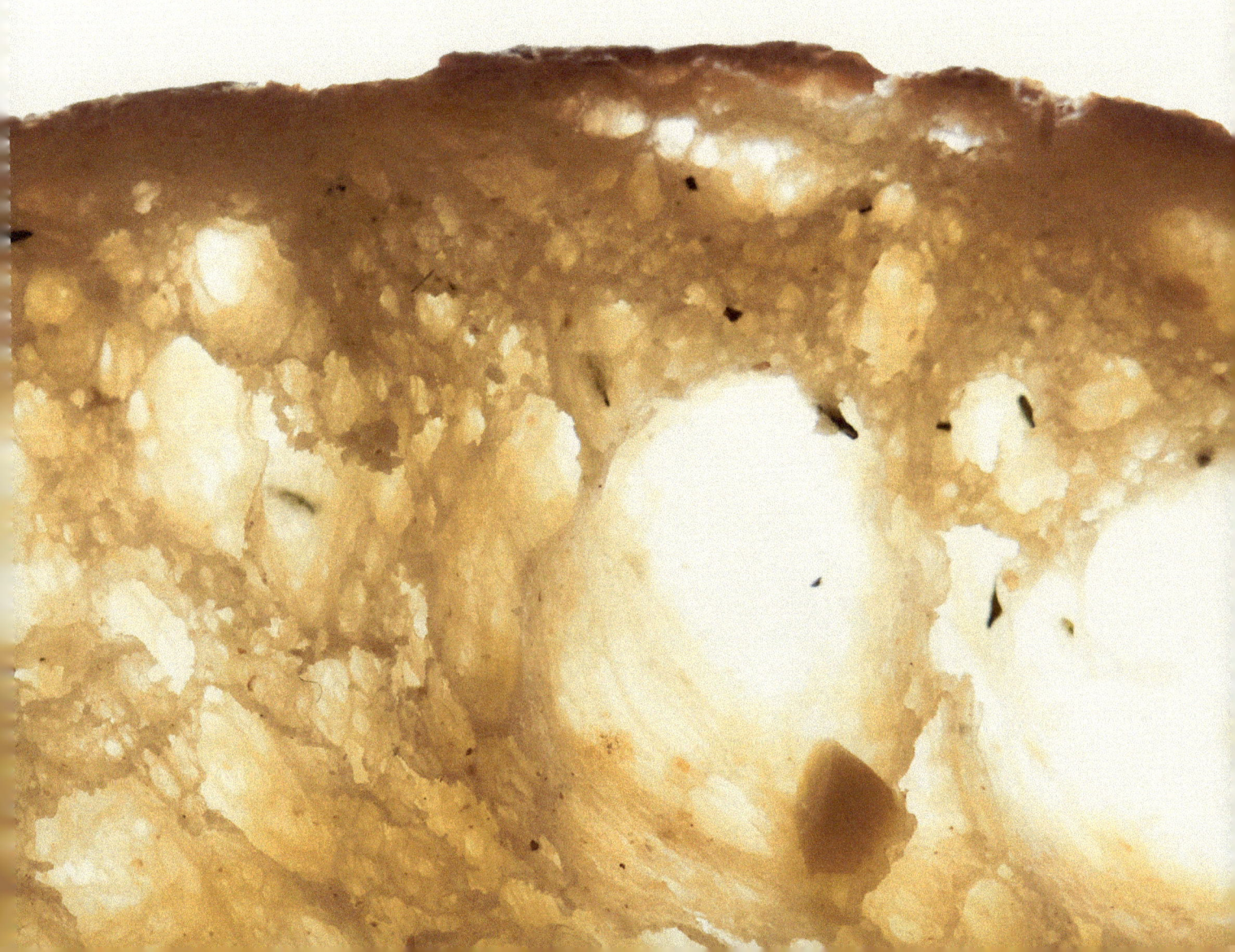

So here we are today, ART IS IN is a bilingual baker's dream-come-true, home to the easy mingling of English and French conversations. Everyone just seems to look happier when they walk through the door—proof that good food really does bring people together. Our reputation was enough to attract Food Network's Guy Fieri to film an episode of *Diners, Drive-ins & Dives.* After a bite of my sesame-crusted sourdough pizza topped with spaghetti and meatballs, Fieri shakes his head and calls me "a dangerous man." He seems genuinely impressed that our pistachio cream stuffed O-Towner (our take on a Cronut, the doughnut-croissant hybrid) is not just Instagrammable but crazy delicious too. "This is a destination doughnut," he said.

"This is a destination doughnut.

Guy Fieri,

Host of Food Network's Diners, Drive-ins and Dives

I began my culinary career making high-end wedding cakes, embellished with fresh flowers and edible gold. But what I do today is about turning every day into a celebration of life. There are no short-cuts at ART IS IN. We make everything from scratch, right down to the ketchup. Yes, our food is photogenic, sometimes dangerously decadent (pulled pork deep fried burger patty, anyone?) and always designed to make you drool-at-first-sight, but it's all about nurturing our cravings, and making every moment as good as it can be—and it's the same recipe I envision for this cookbook. Starting with slow-fermented bread, and expanding into the kitchen, I'm able to share my belief that the small things add up and make a big difference. To me, that's the "art" in ART IS IN. The extra effort of hand-picking the salad greens so you never get a slimy leaf or adding sesame seeds to the pizza crust like a Montreal bagel that's way too good to leave behind. Above all, I believe that mood is a critical ingredient in the kitchen. How you feel, it feeds the food you make, and it gets passed along to the eater. So, I say:

"Be happy—be positive and everything will be dynamite.

— K. Mathieson

THE COOK

This collection of recipes reflects my life.

I've always known I wanted to be a chef and cook for people. And cooking for me is about doing exactly what I want. I want to cook and eat food that's made by hand from scratch, not too fussy, pretty to look at, and packed with flavour. Pizza is truly my obsession—I can't stop making pizza, even when it's my night off or I'm on vacation. And that's one of the things I want to share in this book—not just recipes but an approach to life that leads me to travel and taste and bring it all back into the kitchen to create something one-of-a-kind, like the sourdough pies at ART IS IN. As a chef I soak up new ideas wherever I go. I've honed the ability to scrutinize and deconstruct everything I eat. Whether it's at a bistro in Paris, a bakery in Portland, a taco joint in Mexico City or wood-burning pizza place in Vermont, I love bringing those "taste memories" back to my kitchen (or my backyard pizza oven) where I can recreate and perfect them. Everything we make at the bakery is fuelled by this sense of wanderlust—and this book is a manifesto for scratch cooking.

BOOK

GNOCCHI, PAGE 112

THE ART OF BREAD

CHAPTER 01

THE AUTOLYSE METHOD

Kevin's Tips for Better Bread Making

At Art Is In, we use the autolyse method — a short rest period after combining flour and water, for all of our bread recipes. Because rest is best! This simple pause allows the flour to fully hydrate and then some rather magical changes can occur in your bread dough, including:

01
Gluten bonds begin developing with no effort on the part of the baker. That means kneading and mixing time is reduced.

02
Less time required for mixing means less opportunity for the dough to heat up. Dough temperature is critical for a consistent fermentation process.

03
Fermentation proceeds at a slower pace, allowing for full flavour development and better keeping quality.

04
Carotenoid pigments remain intact, leading to better colour, aroma, and flavour.

05
The dough becomes stretchier, which allows it to expand easily and becomes easier to shape.

THE BEST HOME-BAKED LOAVES

Kevin's Tips for Better Bread Making

Baking bread at home that rivals the quality of loaves from a commercial oven is achievable with a few key tips. Using the following techniques, you can elevate your home-baked bread to bakery-level perfection.

01
Always use the best quality ingredients possible, including unbleached, organic all-purpose flour.

02
If you are adding whole grains to your bread, consider crushing them first. You must also soak them ahead of time. Softer grains will protect the gluten in the bread and lead to a better finished product.

03
Don't punch dough down as many traditional cookbooks suggest. You want to keep the gluten in the bread intact. Similarly, fold it rather than pounding it when kneading.

04
To mimic the steam feature of commercial ovens, which gives bread a dark, chewy crust, preheat a cast iron frying pan for half an hour in a 450° oven. Pour one cup of water into the frying pan when you put your bread in the oven; five minutes later add another cup of water.

05
You should always score the top of your bread before baking (preferably with a razor blade) to allow it to rise higher.

06
A fully baked loaf should feel nice and light, with an evenly browned bottom crust.

POOLISH: DYNAMITE STARTER

Poolish: The Dynamite Bread Starter

In France, bakers traditionally use a preferment or poolish (starter) for making baguettes. We use poolish for our Dynamite bread because it releases the most beautiful flavours and textures. This bread got its name because it explodes in the oven, creating big air pockets under the crust, and it tastes dynamite. It's so much fun to make!

INGREDIENTS

⅔ cup room temperature water
¾ cup all-purpose flour
⅛ tsp fresh yeast

DIRECTIONS

1 Add water to a 1L container and then the yeast and whisk for 20 seconds to combine. Put the whisk away. Add all of the flour at once and use a wooden spoon to mix the poolish until it comes together and there's no dry flour left. Cover it with lightly oiled plastic wrap (or use cooking spray). Leave it for a minimum of 8 hours, or up to 18 hours (overnight) at room temperature. Place it in an area of your kitchen away from heat or cool drafts. Ideally it should be around 25°C (77°F).

2 When the poolish is ready to use, it will have doubled in size, and should look bubbly. That's a sign that it's ripe and ready—it should smell fragrant, fruity like mild banana. I love that smell. If it's not bubbly it means the yeast hasn't activated. Try moving it to a warmer area of the kitchen.

DYNAMITE
WHITE BREAD

Recipe on Next Page

DYNAMITE WHITE BREAD

2 DAY PROCESS | <u>Yield:</u> Makes 3 Large Baguette Loaves

Flavour variations to the dynamite recipe (below): to recreate Art Is In's line of dynamite loaves, add one of the below flavour fillings to the second fold (Step 11) and continue the process.

Roasted Garlic & Rosemary

3 tbsp chopped roasted garlic
1 sprig chopped fresh rosemary

Cheddar Jalapeno

1 cup shredded cheddar
½ cup finely diced jalapenos
5 sprigs finely sliced chives

Kalamata Olive

1 cup kalamata olives

INGREDIENTS

Poolish from page 34
3 ½ cups unbleached flour
1 tbsp sea salt
1 tsp fresh yeast
2 tbsp milk
2 tbsp olive oil
1 ¼ cup water

DIRECTIONS

Day 1

Make the *Poolish*, recipe on page 34.

Day 2

1 Combine water and flour in a mixing bowl and mix slowly for 5 minutes.

2 Cover and allow the mixture to rest for 20 minutes. This rest period, called *Autolyse*, method on page 30, gives the flour time to absorb the liquid.

3 While the dough is resting, add the crumbled yeast, oil, milk and poolish to a seperate bowl.

4 Once the resting period is complete and ingredients from step 3 added, mix slowly for 4 minutes adding the salt halfway through, while the machine is running.

5 Increase mixing to faster speed for 10 minutes while the gluten develops. *The dough will come together and become more elastic. To test this, take a small piece of the dough in your hand and stretch it. If it does not break, the gluten is developed.*

6 Transfer dough into an oiled container. *Rectangular or square shaped will make it easier to shape loaves into a baguette.*

7 Cover the dough with a lid or damp towel and allow it to rest for 90 minutes.

8 After an hour and a half, fold the dough by taking one end of the dough and folding it over towards the center, then take the opposite end and fold it in the same way toward the center.

9 Cover the dough with a lid or damp towel and allow it to rest for 60 minutes.

10 After an hour fold the dough a second time by taking one end of the dough and folding it over towards the center, then take the opposite end and fold it in the same way toward the center.

11 *If you plan to add fillings, fold the fillings in during this fold, then cover the dough with a lid or damp towel and allow it to rest for another 30 minutes.*

12 If you are not adding fillings, cover the dough with a lid or damp towel and allow it to rest for another 30 minutes. It should double in size.

13 Preheat the oven to 475°F.

14 After the dough has rested for 30 minutes dump it from the container onto a floured surface and dust flour over the top.

15 Using your hands, stretch the dough lengthwise until it is even in length at a height of about 2 inches.

16 Cut the dough into desired pieces. Two cuts lengthwise will yield three long baguettes; you can also cut it widthwise to create smaller baguettes or paninis.

17 Place the cut baguettes on parchment-lined baking tray and place on the middle rack of the oven. Place a pan of ice inside the oven to create steam. Bake at 475°F for 6 minutes.

18 Remove the tray of water, reduce heat to 450°F and bake loaves for another 15 minutes until golden and crispy on top and the loaf springs back when you push on the top.

Baking Notes:

Do not bake on the oven floor, make sure you place the loaf on a middle shelf in your oven.

ENGLISH MUFFINS

2 DAY PROCESS | <u>Yield:</u> Makes 12 English Muffins

This is a variation of the *Dynamite Bread* recipe, page 36. To make English muffins, follow the steps from Day 1 and Day 2 steps 1-7 of the dynamite recipe, then follow the below.

INGREDIENTS

In addition to the ingredients used for the dynamite bread recipe:

Semonlina Flour

DIRECTIONS

Following steps 1-7 from the *Dynamite Bread* recipe, page 36.

1 Once the dough has been mixed and has rested, cut it into 80g portions and form into rounds.

2 Cover with a clean damp cloth and let rest for 30 minutes.

3 Bring a flat griddle or frying pan to medium, oil the pan and sprinkle a light dusting of semolina on the pan before laying your dough rounds on top. Cook tor 3 minutes on each side making sure to sprinkle more semolina in between sides. The semolina will help you get a nice crispy crust.

MOTHER SOURDOUGH STARTER

4 DAY PROCESS (ONGOING) | To be used with our sourdough recipes.

INGREDIENTS

Organic Whole Wheat Flour
Water

Baking Notes:

It's best to use organic flour because it has a higher sugar content.

DIRECTIONS

Day 1

Start by mixing two parts organic whole wheat flour, one part room temperature water. Mix in a jar, cover with a cheese cloth and store in a room temperature, dark place. The kitchen cupboard is perfect.

Day 2

After a couple of days at room temperature, it will begin to bubble. This means it's creating bacteria and activating. Once it starts to bubble, feed your mother daily. Mix 180g flour and 144ml room temperature water into the mother.

Day 3

Keep 180g of mother and discard the rest. Feed with 180g of flour and 144ml of water.

Day 4

Keep 180g of mother and discard the rest. Feed with 180g of flour and 144ml of water.

After About A Week

After about one week you will see it has been bubbling and growing. You are ready to begin using it.

Make sure it is bubbly and active before feeding, it should double in size between feedings.

At this point you can store it in the fridge and only feed it every couple of days.

To use your mother in the levain, remove it from the refrigerator the day before, feed it and let it sit out. It should double in size.

To keep your mother alive, make sure there is some left over after using it and continue your regular feeding schedule. If you want to increase your mother, don't discard.

KEVIN'S WHITE SOURDOUGH

Recipe on Next Page

KEVIN'S WHITE SOURDOUGH

3 DAY PROCESS | <u>Yield</u>: Makes 2 800g Loaves

INGREDIENTS

Levain

⅔ cup room temp. water
¾ cup all-purpose flour
1 ½ tbsps *Mother*, page 40

Dough

4 ¾ cups all-purpose flour
¼ cup whole wheat flour
1 tbsp sea salt
1 tbsp fresh yeast
Levain from Day 1
2 ¾ cups water

DIRECTIONS

Day 1

Make the *Levain*. Should be made 8 to 18 hours in advance. Mix levain ingredients together, cover and let rest for at least 8 hours or overnight at room temperature.

Day 2

1 To make the dough: combine water, levain from day 1, and flour to a mixing bowl and mix on low speed with a dough hook for 4 minutes to combine.

2 Cover and allow the mixture to *autolyze* for 15 minutes to give the flour time to absorb the liquid. While the dough rests, add crumbled yeast to the bowl.

3 Mix on slow for 4 minutes. Add the salt halfway through.

4 Turn on mixer to medium speed and mix for 15-20 minutes. Stop the machine once the dough comes together and starts to slap around in the bowl. A few points to keep in mind; do not let your dough get warm while mixing it. If it does get warm, reduce the speed, and only mix another 2-3 minutes.

A good indication that the dough is ready is the elasticity. You will notice the dough is smooth and shiny. Stop mixing and test this by pulling a small piece of dough; if it stretches without tearing, it has built enough strength. If it rips easily, keep mixing. It should also have come off the edges of the bowl forming a ball and slapping around the bowl when mixing.

5 Transfer the dough to an oiled plastic container with a lid or damp towel and allow it to rest for 60 minutes.

6 After 60 minutes, fold the dough by taking one end of the dough and folding it over towards the center, then take the opposite end and fold it in the same way toward the center.

7 Cover the dough with a lid or damp towel and allow it to rest for 60 minutes.

8 After 60 minutes, fold the dough by taking one end of the dough and folding it over towards the center, then take the opposite end and fold it in the same way toward the center.

9 Cover the dough with a lid or damp towel and allow it to rest for 30 to 60 minutes.

10 After 30-60 minutes the dough should be slack. Dump out onto floured surface and cut in half to make 2 loaves. Preshape the dough into rounds by tucking corners into the center and flipping over to round it off.

11 Let it rest for 15- 30 min.

12 After 15-30 minutes it's time for the final shape. Flip the dough ball over and take the sides of the dough and fold into the center. Take the end closest to you and fold forward over the center and tighten loaf against table surface. You should end up with an oval loaf that's tough and bouncy.

13 Place your dough ball into an oiled 5x10x 3" bread pan and let it proof at room temperature for 1 hour to kick start the process. Finish proofing overnight in the fridge.

Day 3

1 Preheat oven to 450°F. Place a larger roasting pan (Cast iron or Dutch oven large enough to fit the 2 loaf pans inside) into the oven to heat up.

2 Remove loaves from fridge 20-30 minutes before baking, they should have risen about a half inch above the lip of the pan. The loaves should still be cold when they go in the oven.

3 Lightly dust your loaves with flour, making sure it's completely coated with a THIN layer of flour.

4 Use a razor blade or a sharp knife, score the top with your preferred design.

5 Place the loaf pans inside the roasting pan and surround the loaf pans with ice to create steam. This should be done quickly without removing the roasting pan or keeping the oven door open for too long.

6 Bake at 500°F for 10 minutes

7 Reduce heat to 420°F and bake for another 30 minutes.

8 Check your bread, look for a golden brown or deep amber colour. Test the readiness by removing it from the pan and tapping the bottom. It should sound hollow if it's ready.If it's not, add another 10 minutes baking time.

9 Once it is done let it cool completely on a wire rack before cutting.

PIZZA DOUGH BALL

3 DAY PROCESS | This is a variation of the *Kevin's White Sourdough* recipe, page 44.

INGREDIENTS

In addition to the ingredients used for White Sourdough:

Semonlina Flour

DIRECTIONS

Following Day 2, Steps 1-6 from the *Kevin's White Sourdough* recipe, page 44:

1 Once the dough has been mixed and has rested, cut it into 300g portions and form into rounds.

2 Coat your dough rounds with a dusting of a 50/50 mixture of flour and semolina and let it rest for 30 minutes.

3 Now your sourdough pizza is ready to be shaped. Find our Pizza Dough Technique on page 120.

HERB & CHEESE SOURDOUGH

3 DAY PROCESS | This is a variation of the *Kevin's White Sourdough* recipe, page 44.

INGREDIENTS

In addition to the ingredients used for White Sourdough:

1 cup shredded cheddar

5 chives sprigs, chopped

¼ raw onion, chopped

DIRECTIONS

Following Day 2, Steps 1-6 from the *Kevin's White Sourdough* recipe, page 44:

1 Add the filling ingredients to the first fold (Day 2, step 6), and then continue to follow to the end of the recipe.

ROSEMARY & GARLIC SOURDOUGH

3 DAY PROCESS | This is a variation of the *Kevin's White Sourdough* recipe, page 44.

INGREDIENTS

In addition to the ingredients used for White Sourdough:

- ⅛ cup roasted garlic (mashed)
- 2 sprigs chopped rosemary

DIRECTIONS

Following Day 2, Steps 1-6 from the *Kevin's White Sourdough* recipe, page 44:

1 Add the filling ingredients to the first fold (Day 2, step 6), and then continue to follow to the end of the recipe.

WHOLE WHEAT & RYE SOURDOUGH

3 DAY PROCESS | This is a variation of the *Kevin's White Sourdough* recipe, page 44.

INGREDIENTS

5 ½ cups whole wheat flour
¼ cup rye flour
1 tbsp sea salt
1 tsp fresh yeast
1 ½ cups *Levain*
3 cups water

Levain

¾ cup water (room temp)
1 ½ cups all-purpose flour
¾ cup *Mother,* page 40

DIRECTIONS

Follow the directions for the Kevin's white sourdough recipe, page 44. Use the ingredients listed here instead of the original ones for the whole wheat and rye variation, and then continue to follow to the end of the recipe.

RAISIN SOURDOUGH

3 DAY PROCESS | This is a variation of the *Kevin's White Sourdough* recipe, page 44.

INGREDIENTS

5 cups whole wheat flour
¼ cup rye flour
¾ tbsp sea salt
1 tsp fresh yeast
1 cup *Levain*
2 ½ cups water
1 cup raisins

Levain

¾ cup water (room temp)
1 ½ cups all-purpose flour
¾ cup *Mother*, page 40

DIRECTIONS

Follow the directions for the Kevin's white sourdough recipe, page 44. Add the filling ingredients to the first fold (Day 2, Step 6). Use the ingredients listed here instead of the original ones for the whole wheat and rye variation, and then continue to follow to the end of the recipe.

BUTTERMILK MULTISEED BREAD

3 DAY PROCESS | **Yield:** Makes 2 800g Loaves

INGREDIENTS (DAY 1)

Poolish
½ cup + 1 tbsp room temp water
¼ cup all purpose flour
1 tsp fresh yeast

Multi-Seed Mix
¼ cup flax seeds
¼ cup sunflower seeds
¼ cup sesame seeds
¼ cup cornmeal
Pinch of poppy seeds

DIRECTIONS

Day 1

1 Make the *Poolish* by combining ingredients listed, recipe steps on page 34. It should be made 8 to 18 hours in advance.

2 Make the multi-seed mix. Combine all the ingredients of the buttermilk multiseed mixture together in an airtight container. This can be stored for up to 90 days so a large batch can be made well in advance and used as needed.

INGREDIENTS (DAY 2)

Part A
¾ cup + 2 tbsp of water
¾ cup buttermilk
¼ cup honey
Poolish, page 34
¼ cup of cooked brown rice

Part B
2 tbsp fresh yeast

Part C
3 ½ cups all-purpose flour
4 tbsp wholewheat flour
1 cup multi-seed mix
1 tbsp sea salt
¼ cup brown sugar

Day 2

1 To make the dough: combine all the ingredients in part A together in a mixing bowl.

2 Add the yeast (part B).

3 Add the dry ingredients (part C). The salt should go in last.

4 Using a dough hook, mix on low speed for 4 mins.

5 Increase mixing speed to high and mix for another 8-15 minutes or until the dough comes together and it starts to slap around in the bowl. The dough will have an elastic feeling when it's finished mixing.

6 Place the dough into an oiled container, cover and let rest for 60 minutes.

7 After an hour, fold the dough by taking one end of the dough and folding it over towards the center, then take the opposite end and fold it in the same way towards the center. Cover the dough and let rest for 45 minutes.

8 After 45 minutes the dough should be slack. Dump out onto floured surface and cut in half to make 2 loaves. Preshape the dough into rounds by tucking corners into the center and flipping over to round it off. Let it rest for 15- 30 minutes.

9 After 15-30 minutes it's time for the final shape. Flip the dough ball over and take the sides of the dough and fold into the center. Take the end closest to you and fold forward over the center and tighten loaf against table surface. You should end up with an oval loaf that's tough and bouncy.

10 Place 3 cups of sunflower seeds in a shallow dish and set aside. Roll your shaped loaf over a clean, damp kitchen cloth to moisten the surface, then evenly coat it by rolling it in the sesame seeds.

11 Place your dough balls seam side down into an oiled 5x10x3 bread pan and let it proof at room temperature for 1 hour to kick start the process. Finish proofing overnight in the fridge.

Day 3

1 Preheat oven to 450°F. Place a larger roasting pan (cast iron or Dutch oven large enough to fit the 2 loaf pans inside) into the oven to heat up.

2 Remove loaves from fridge 15 to 20 minutes before baking, it should have risen about a half inch above the lip of the pan. The loaves should still be cold when they go in the oven.

3 Place the loaf pans inside the roasting pan & surround the loaf pans with ice to create steam. *This should be done quickly without removing the roasting pan or keeping the oven door open for too long.*

4 Bake at 450°F for 10 minutes. Reduce heat to 350°F, remove the ice trays from the oven, and bake for another 40 minutes.

5 Check your bread, look for a golden brown or deep amber colour. Test the readiness by removing it from the pan and tapping the bottom. It should sound hollow if it's ready. If it's not, add another 5 minutes baking time.

6 Once it is done, let it cool completely on a wire rack before cutting.

CRAZY GRAIN BREAD

Recipe on Next Page

BEEF BRISKET TOURTIÈRE

Yield: Makes 2 Tourtières

INGREDIENTS

Pâte Brisée Dough, page 176
(Double this recipe for two pies)

1 kg beef brisket
2 tbsps sea salt
1 tbsp black pepper
2 white onions
3 carrots
3 tbsps olive oil
2 tbsps sea salt
3 tbsps crushed garlic
3 tbsps flour
¼ cup tomato paste
¾ cup red wine
1 cup cheese curds
1 cup mashed potatoes
1 egg
1 tbsp water

DIRECTIONS

1 Preheat your oven to 500°F. Rub the brisket with olive oil, salt, and pepper.

2 Place it on a baking pan or dish and roast for 25 minutes or until it is nicely browned.

3 Take it out of the oven and let cool. Keep the roasting pan aside for later.

4 Place the olive oil, onions, and salt in a pot. Start cooking on high heat until it starts to sweat and have a golden color.

5 Turn off the heat and add your crushed garlic and flour, mixing until combined.

6 Place the onion mixture in the roasting pan and add the red wine.

7 Rub the brisket in tomato paste and place it in the roasting pan.

8 Cover the brisket with parchment paper and tightly wrap with double tin foil.

9 Bake it at 220°F for 8 hours. This can be done overnight.

10 Once cooked, remove the brisket, and set it on a cooling tray. Strain the liquid for later use, and adjust the seasoning.

11 Cut the brisket into small cubes and mix in the reserved liquid. Mix well and put aside. Preheat your oven to 375°F.

12 Using your double recipe of *Pâte Brisée*, divide your dough into four balls — one for the bottom, and one for the top of each pie. Roll out the bottoms to ¼" thickness and fit into your pie shells.

13 Fill your two pie bases with 1 cup mashed potatoes, 1 cup cheese curds, and half of the meat mixture. You should have enough to make 2 tourtières.

14 Roll out the tops to ½" thickness, then egg wash the contour of your pie for the lid to stick. Add your pâte brisée lids on top of the filled pie shells. Make a few holes on your lid to let steam out while baking.

15 Press the edges of your base and lid together. Press again with the legs of a fork to make sure it is nice and tightly closed.

16 Egg wash the top of your pie and let it dry for 10 minutes. Add another layer of egg wash.

17 Bake your tourtière at 375°F for 45 minutes, until the crust is golden. Let it cool at least 15 minutes before serving.

KEVIN'S MEATBALLS

Yield: Makes 20 Meatballs

INGREDIENTS

1 ¾ cups ground beef

1 ¾ cups ground pork

2 whole eggs

1 cup Pecorino Romano cheese

½ cup chopped parsley

½ tsp crushed garlic

a pinch black pepper

1 ½ cups breadcrumbs

1 tbsp sea salt

1 ½ cups cold water

DIRECTIONS

1 In a mixing bowl, combine all the ingredients except the water. Mix on low speed, gradually adding the water. Stop mixing once the water is fully incorporated.

2 Take care not to over mix. Maximum 3 minutes.

3 Prepare an oven tray with parchment paper, preheat your oven to 375°F.

4 Make the balls using an ice cream scoop, about 2 ounces each. Set them on your oven tray.

5 Bake your meatballs for 20 minutes.

6 We like our meatballs with our *Nonna Sauce* page 114, and grated mozzarella, then bake again at 375°F to melt the cheese.

> **I translate childhood memories into the foods I create.**
>
> — Chef Kevin Mathieson

GNOCCHI

Yield: Makes 6 Portions

INGREDIENTS

6 large potatoes, unpeeled

6 egg yolks

¼ cup parmesan

1 tbsp salt

1 ½ cups flour

semolina & flour, to dust surface

DIRECTIONS

1 Pierce whole potatoes all over with a fork, then bake at 350°F for 1 hour or until soft.

2 While the potatoes are still warm, cut them in half and scoop out the flesh. Pass the flesh through a vegetable mill or grate it using the large holes of a cheese grater to create a mash.

3 Combine the potato mash, egg yolks, and parmesan in a mixing bowl. Mix using a paddle attachment until well combined. Then, gradually add the salt and flour on low speed until the mixture comes together.

4 Prepare a baking tray sprinkled with semolina and set aside.

5 Place the dough on a floured work surface and knead until smooth. If the dough is wet or sticky, add flour a little at a time until it reaches a smooth, non-sticky texture.

6 Divide the dough in half to create more manageable pieces. Roll each piece into a snake-like shape, ensuring each has a 1-inch diameter. Cut the dough into 1-inch pieces to form your gnocchi. Place the cut gnocchi on the prepared semolina tray to prevent sticking.

7 Bring a medium pot of salty water to a boil. Once boiling, add your gnocchi in batches to cook them. They will need about 2-3 minutes, and they will float when they are ready.

8 If you are using them right away, toss them with some olive oil and serve with your choice of sauce. We like baking them in the oven at 375°F with our *Nonna Sauce* page 114 and parmesan for 10 minutes!

9 If you plan to serve the gnocchi later, drop them into ice water after boiling to stop the cooking process. Strain them and toss in some olive oil to prevent sticking.

Storage: The gnocchi can be kept in an airtight container in your fridge for up to 3 days. They freeze well for up to 3 weeks.

GNOCCHI-MAKING TECHNIQUE

NONNA SAUCE

Yield: Makes 1L Sauce

INGREDIENTS

4 ½ cups whole peeled tomatoes
½ cup diced butter
1 whole onion
2 tsp of salt

DIRECTIONS

1 Prepare your onion by cutting it in half and peeling the skin off.

2 In a medium saucepan, combine all ingredients and gently simmer for two hours on medium heat. This will allow the flavours to meld and develop.

3 After simmering, remove and discard the onions as they will have infused all of their flavours into the sauce.

4 We aren't looking for a smooth sauce, however you can use a hand blender to give it a slightly chunky texture.

Storage: Let the sauce cool at room temperature before putting it in an airtight container in the fridge. Can be kept for up to 5 days.

MAC & CHEESE SAUCE

Yield: Makes 2.5L of Sauce

INGREDIENTS

¾ cup diced butter
1 cup all-purpose flour
4 ½ cups milk
1 tsp dry mustard powder
1 bay leaf
1 tbsp sea salt
¼ tsp nutmeg
1 tsp onion powder
2 ½ cups cheddar cheese
⅓ cup milk

DIRECTIONS

1 In a medium saucepan, heat up the 4 ½ cups of milk with all the spices.

2 In a separate saucepan, melt the butter. Once melted, add the flour while stirring with a spatula to make a roux.

3 When the roux and spice mixture has come to a boil, add in ⅓ of the spiced milk on medium heat whisking vigorously to prevent lumps. Then add ⅓ more and mix well to combine, it should thicken right away. Add the rest of the milk and bring it to a boil once again. Then remove from heat.

4 Add the cheese to the sauce, and mix well to combine.

5 Finally, finish by adding ⅓ cup of milk and season to taste.

6 Cover the warm cheese sauce with a plastic cover touching the sauce, preventing a crust from forming, and refrigerate.

Storage: Can be kept in the fridge for up to 4 days.

"

Whether it's at a bistro in Paris, a bakery in Portland, a taco joint in Mexico City or wood-burning pizza place in Vermont, I love bringing those "taste memories" back to my kitchen.

— Chef Kevin Mathieson

THE ART OF PIZZA

PIZZA DOUGH SHAPING

Yield: Makes 1 Pizza | Use our *Pizza Dough Ball* recipe to create your pizzas, page 46.

INGREDIENTS

Pizza Dough Ball, page 46
sesame seeds
flour
semolina
garlic infused olive oil

Tools

a brush
a scraper (plastic or metal)
a circular pizza tray
a pizza pan

DIRECTIONS

1 Your dough should be at room temperature before you start stretching it. If it is too cold, it will not cooperate when you try to stretch it. *If you feel resistance in the dough let it rest 10 minutes and try again.*

2 Prepare your pizza pan by lightly oiling it and applying a thin layer of semolina. Set your pan aside while you stretch your dough.

3 Dust your prep surface with some semolina before placing your dough, sticky side down on top. Pat the dough down using your fingers from the middle going outwards always keeping it in a circular shape as evenly as you can until it is 1" thick. Use more semolina if it's sticky.

4 Once your dough has started widening, pick it up and start stretching it with your knuckles. Try to avoid manipulating your dough with your fingers, which can create holes in your dough. Do this by placing your knuckles as close to the edge as you can and gently stretching the dough allowing gravity to pull the dough down while your carefully rotate the dough going around, keeping the edges slightly thicker to create a crust until it's the right size, about 12". Your dough should be very thin, almost see through.

5 Place your dough on your pizza tray.

6 Using your brush, gently apply a thin layer of garlic oil around the edges of your crust and sprinkle with a generous amount of sesame seeds.

7 Now you are ready to build your pizza. You can top your pizza with any of your favourite ingredients, or try some of the Art Is In customer favourites.

PIZZA DOUGH MAKING TECHNIQUE

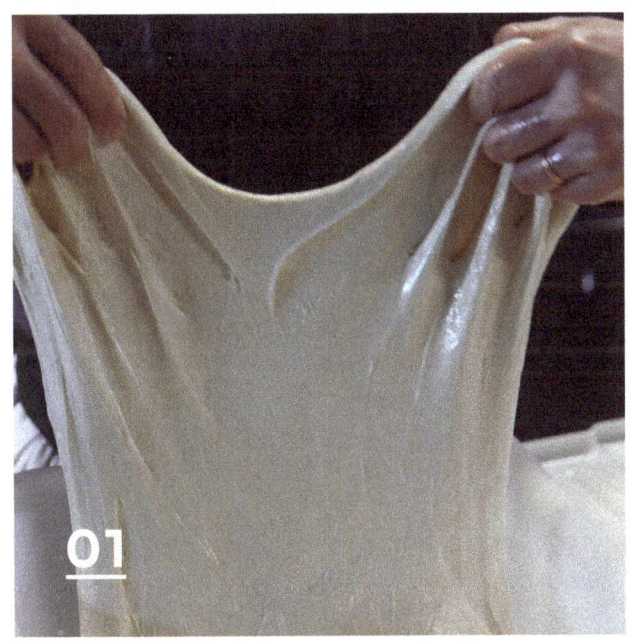

01

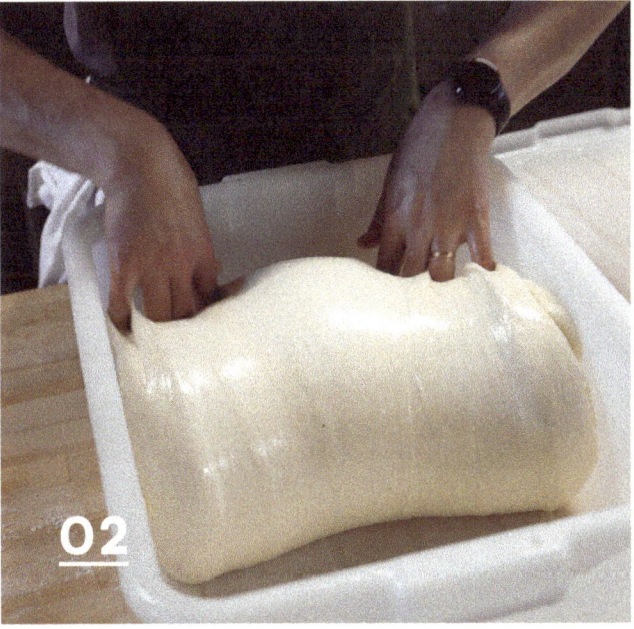

02

05

06

Whether you're a seasoned cook or new to pizza-making, these steps will help you achieve a delicious, crispy crust. Don't forget, always let your dough warm to room temperature before starting — and preheat your oven to 500 degrees for all of our pizza recipes!

Pizza Dough Recipe — Previous Page
Kevin's Pizza Sauce Recipe — Next Page

KEVIN'S PIZZA SAUCE

Yield: Makes 1L of Sauce

INGREDIENTS

1 ½ cups whole peeled tomatoes, canned
1 tbsp crushed garlic
1 fresh thyme spring
2 tbsps olive oil
¼ of a white onion
1 tbsp fresh basil
a pinch salt
a pinch pepper

DIRECTIONS

1 Roughly chop the onion and crush the garlic.

2 In a medium saucepan, heat the olive oil and sweat the onion, garlic, and thyme over medium heat until the onion is translucent.

3 Add tomatoes with their juice, bring to a simmer and cook for 30 minutes.

4 Take off the heat and blend all the ingredients with an immersion blender. Don't make a smooth paste, small chunks are what we want.

5 Chop your fresh basil and add it to the sauce, season to taste.

Storage: Refrigerate in an airtight container for up to 7 days.

PARMESAN DIP

Yield: Makes 2 ½ Cups of Dip

INGREDIENTS

2 cups *House Mayo, page 84*
¼ cup + 1 tbsp red wine vinegar
1 tsp crushed garlic
1 tsp dried oregano
1 cup grated parmesan
a pinch sea salt

DIRECTIONS

1 Mix all ingredients in a bowl with a whisk until combined.

Storage: Store in the fridge in an air-tight container for up to 5 days.

CHEESE LOUISE

Yield: Makes 1 Pizza | Preheat your oven to 500°F for all pizza recipes.

INGREDIENTS

1 *Pizza Dough* base, page 120
⅓ cup *Kevin's Pizza Sauce*, page 124
1 cup grated mozzarella cheese
8 leaves fresh basil
Romano parmesan cheese, to dust

DIRECTIONS

1 Pour the pizza sauce into the middle of the dough and use the back of a spoon to spread it out and around your dough until it is about ¼" away from the edge.

2 Sprinkle the mozzarella cheese in an even layer over the surface.

3 Bake your pizza in a 500°F oven for 7 minutes, rotate your pizza, lower to 180°F and cook for another 4 minutes. You want your cheese melted and your crust slightly charred but not over cooked.

4 Remove your pizza from the oven and top with the fresh basil leaves, and dust with Romano parmesan cheese.

THE ART OF PASTRY

CHAPTER 05

CHEWY CHOCOLATE WALNUT COOKIES

I first discovered these glossy, crackly, fudgey cookies when I was working at Payard Patisserie & Bistro in New York nearly two decades ago. Payard, who is credited as the inventor of this commonly recreated confection, said he was inspired by the features of a French macaron, with its chewy interior and a crisp meringue-like outer shell. But imagine crossing that quintessentially delicate French treat with the amplified decadence of an American chunky chocolate-chip cookie or a gooey dark chocolate brownie. That's pure Payard genius.

These beloved cookies, which happen to satisfy a wide range of diets thanks to being flourless, gluten- and dairy-free, have become an Ottawa favourites since I introduced them in 2006. We still make dozens of them every day. In order to get the ultimate shiny, crackly surface with the desired gooey middle, we make them in a convection oven which helps them to melt perfectly, but a regular oven is fine. —K.M

INGREDIENTS

7 egg whites
5 tbsps vanilla extract
5 cups icing sugar
1 cups cocoa powder
1 tsp salt
5 cups chopped walnuts

DIRECTIONS

1 Preheat your oven to 375°F.

2 Line a baking sheet with parchment paper.

3 Place all the ingredients into a mixing bowl. Walnuts should go in last.

4 Mix on low speed until all the ingredients are incorporated. Be careful not to overmix, the batter should be incorporated and shiny, not like whipped egg whites.

5 Use a 2oz scoop to scoop the mixture onto your prepared baking sheet leaving about 2" space between each cookie.

6 Bake at 375°F for 17 minutes. You'll know it's baked when the cookies begin to crackle on top.

PEANUT BUTTER COOKIES

Yield: Makes 12 Cookies

INGREDIENTS

Part A
½ cup peanut butter
½ cup soft butter
¾ cup brown sugar
¾ cup granulated sugar

Part B
2 eggs, room temperature
1 tsp vanilla

Part C
⅓ cup all-purpose flour
1 ⅓ cups pastry flour
½ tsp baking soda
a pinch salt

Part D
1 ¼ cups milk chocolate chunks
⅔ cup roasted peanuts

DIRECTIONS

1 Preheat your oven to 375°F.

2 Line a baking sheet with parchment paper.

3 Cream together the ingredients in part A, scrape the bottom of the bowl to ensure everything is well incorporated.

4 In a separate bowl, mix the ingredients in part B and add half to the mixer with part A making sure to get it all combined. Add the other half and make sure it's well incorporated, scrape the bottom of the bowl to make sure it is well mixed.

5 Once the mixture looks homogenous, add in the ingredients of part C, mix. Don't forget to scrape the bottom of the bowl.

6 Mix in the ingredients of part D.

7 Using a 2oz scoop, scoop the mixture onto your prepared baking sheet leaving about 2" space between each cookie. Use the palm of your hand to slightly flatten the cookies.

8 Place your tray of cookies in the freezer for a half hour before baking. *It's crucial for the cookie dough to be cold when it goes into the oven. This will ensure chewy cookies.*

9 Bake at 375°F for 16 minutes until the edges are golden.

FINANCIERS

Yield: Makes 20 Cookies

INGREDIENTS

⅓ cup *Brown Butter*
1 ¼ cups granulated sugar
¾ cup + 2 tbsp almond flour
¾ cup pastry flour
8 egg whites
1 tsp baking powder
¾ cup melted butter
1 tsp vanilla

DIRECTIONS

Brown Butter

1 Add ⅓ of a cup of butter into a pan with a light coloured bottom (this will allow you to see the browning as it progresses) and heat.

2 Once the butter is melted and begins to boil, reduce the heat to medium and let the butter simmer until foamy.

3 Continue cooking while stirring and scraping the bottom of the pan until the foam begins to subside and the butter becomes golden brown with a nutty aroma.

4 Remove from the heat immediately and pour it out of the pan to avoid burning.

Financier Batter

1 Preheat the oven to 375°F.

2 Prepare financier molds with butter or nonstick spray so the batter won't stick.

3 Add the freshly made brown butter to the melted butter and set aside.

4 Add the egg whites and vanilla to the bowl with the dry ingredients. Mix well making sure to scrape the bottom and sides of the bowl.

5 Slowly pour the butter blend to the mixture to create an emulsion.

6 Let the mixture in the fridge for 30 minutes before pouring into the molds.

7 Pour the batter into the molds.

8 Bake at 375°F for 16 minutes until golden.

MACARONS

Recipe on Next Page

MACARONS

Yield: Makes 33-35 Macarons

We use this recipe as a base to make all our flavours. This is done by adding oil-based food colouring to achieve your colour of choice. This is optional!

INGREDIENTS

Part A: Italian Meringue

2 egg whites
½ cup granulated sugar
¼ cup water

Part B: Icing

1 cup almond flour
1 cup icing sugar
2 tbsp icing sugar
1 egg white

Baking Notes:

You want to make sure your egg whites are foamy before adding your hot syrup. The meringue will be shiny and glossy, this can be best achieved using a hand mixer.

DIRECTIONS

1 Preheat oven to 350°F.

2 Make an Italian butter cream: In a mixing bowl, whip your egg whites from part A until they have soft peaks. Set it aside.

3 In a small pot, combine granulated sugar and water of Part A together and simmer over medium heat. Cook until it reaches 119-200°C. To prevent crystallization, it's important to avoid mixing the sugar as it heats. It's a good idea to brush sides of the pan with a humid brush, just be careful not to add water to the mixture.

4 Once you have reached the temperature, slowly pour your hot sugar into the soft peak egg whites while mixing. Once you are done pouring, keep mixing your meringue until it has completely cooled down. It should be shiny, thick and have firm peaks when you remove your whisk.

5 In a seperate bowl, combine the ingredients of Part B together and mix until it forms a paste. You can use your hands.

6 Incorporate ¼ of the meringue into the paste using a spatula. Do so very gently as you do not want to break the air built up in the meringue.

7 Continue slowly adding the meringue in quarters; you are looking for a thick, creamy, and fluffy mix. You can check this by putting a spatula in your mix and lifting it out. The mix on the end of the spatula should form a V shape and remain on the spatula. If it is continually dripping, your mix has lost too much air and it will cause the top of your macarons to crack.

8 Add 3-4 drops of oil-based food coloring of your choice. Do not over mix.

9 To get even macarons, take a piece of parchment paper and trace 1.25" to 1.5" circles with a permanent marker off the lid of a bottle or another item that has your desired size. Place it on an oven tray and cover it with new parchment paper.

10 Place your macaron mix into a pipping bag with a small pipping tip. Start pipping your macaron over the circles. Leave a bit of space between the macarons as they will spread and expand a bit. Let the top layer of the macarons dry to the touch before putting them in the oven. If they are too wet, they will not bake evenly.

11 Bake at 350°F (or 320° on fan convection) for 10 minutes. You want to have a bit of browning around the edges, a smooth surface, a colored bottom, and a chewy inside.

12 Let them cool at room temperature before filling a bottom cookie and topping it with another cookie.

Macaron Filling Options

1 For the vanilla macaron, use a plain cookie recipe filled with *White Chocolate Filling*, recipe on page 150.

2 For the chocolate macaron, add 3 drops of brown food coloring to the cookie filled with *Chocolate Crèmeux*, recipe on page 151.

3 For the raspberry macaron, add 3-4 drops of red or pink food coloring to the cookie filled with *Raspberry Jam*, recipe on page 172.

Storage: Once filled, the macarons should be stored in an airtight container in your freezer for up to 2 weeks. This will keep them fresh and prevent them from getting soggy in the fridge. Pull them out of the freezer 15 minutes before serving.

CHOCOLATE ESPRESSO BROWNIES

Yield: Makes 15 Brownies

INGREDIENTS

3 ⅓ cups brown sugar
1 ¼ cups butter
4 room temperature eggs
a double shot espresso (cold)
1 tsp vanilla
¾ cup cocoa powder
¾ cup pastry flour
¾ cup bakery flour
½ tsp baking soda
¾ cups chocolate pieces (64%)

Baking Notes:

You can check if it is fully baked by poking the center with a paring knife or toothpick. If it comes out clean it is baked, if not, put it back in for a few more minutes.

DIRECTIONS

1 Preheat your oven to 375°F. *Make sure the fan is on in your oven.*

2 Prepare your baking pan by spraying it with cooking spray, lining with parchment paper, and setting aside.

3 In a mixing bowl, cream together butter and brown sugar until fluffy. Scrape the sides and bottom of the bowl to ensure it is well combined.

4 While the mixer is on low, add the eggs one by one until incorporated.

5 Add the cooled espresso and vanilla. Do not forget to scrape the sides of the bowl so it is well combined.

6 Add the dry ingredients to the bowl and mix lightly. Before the batter is fully combined, add the chocolate pieces and continue to mix until just combined.

7 Pour the batter into your parchment lined baking 10x 12" dish and use an offset spatula to spread the batter evenly.

8 Bake at 375°F for 45 minutes or until cooked through.

Chocolate Ganache Topping

- 1 ½ cups cream (35%)
- 1 ¾ cups chocolate pieces (50%)
- 1 tsp trimoline or glucose
- 2 tbsps soft butter

1 Prepare your mise en place by combining the chocolate and trimoline (or glucose) together in a bowl, set your soft butter aside and put your cream into a saucepan.

2 Slowly bring the cream to a boil over medium high heat, being careful not to burn it.

3 Once the cream is boiling, remove it from the heat and pour it over your chocolate pieces. Let it stand for 1-2 minutes for the cream to begin melting the chocolate.

4 Slowly stir your cream and chocolate mixture starting from the middle out to the sides of the bowl.

5 Once it's about 50% mixed add the butter and continue to stir until fully combined.

6 Place a layer of saran wrap directly over the ganache to prevent contact from the air. Let the mixture cool at room temperature.

7 Once the brownies and ganache are fully cooled, spread a thick layer of ganache over the top of the brownies. Dust the top with cocoa powder and cut into even pieces. *Ganache can be made the night before, but must not be refrigerated or it will get too hard.*

WHITE CHOCOLATE FILLING

This can be used to fill the *Macarons*, recipe on page 146.

INGREDIENTS

¼ cup of sugar
⅓ cup + 2 tbsp cream (35%)
a splash vanilla extract
2 tbsps cornstarch
¼ cup diced butter
⅓ cup white chocolate pieces

DIRECTIONS

1 In a bowl, combine the cornstarch and the 2 tbsp of cream and set aside.

2 Place the butter and the white chocolate In a separate bowl.

3 In a saucepan, bring the remaining cream, sugar, and vanilla to a boil stirring it with a spatula to avoid burning.

4 Once the cream and sugar have come to a boil, pour half into the cornstarch mix, and whisk well until combined. Then add the remaining hot cream mixture.

5 Pour the warm cream mixture onto the butter and chocolate and let melt. Mix until combined.

6 Place in the fridge overnight or until cooled. Once cooled, whip the mixture until light and fluffy.

7 Put the filling into a piping bag with a small piping tip to fill your macarons.

CHOCOLATE CRÉMEUX

This can be used to fill the *Macarons*, recipe on page 146.

INGREDIENTS

1 cup + 2 tbsp milk
1 cup + 2 tbsp cream
9 egg yolks
3 ½ tbsps granulated sugar
¼ cup milk chocolate chunks
1 ½ cups dark chocolate chunks

Baking Notes:

Tempering is a technique used in cooking to stabilize ingredients by slowing heating and cooling them.

DIRECTIONS

1 Measure chocolate into large bowl and set aside.

2 In a saucepan on medium heat, bring the milk and cream to a boil.

3 In a separate bowl, mix sugar and eggs together.

4 Temper eggs with milk and cream.

5 Return to stove and bring up to 85°C.

6 Pour into fine mesh sieve over chocolate.

7 Finish mixing your crémeux with an immersion blender to achieve a smooth cream.

BUTTER CROISSANTS

Recipe on Next Page

BUTTER CROISSANTS

3 DAY PROCESS

This recipe is your base for making many different *viennoiserie* (pastries). This recipe can be used to make *Chocolate Croissants* page 156, ham & cheese croissants, and danishes.

INGREDIENTS

Dough

¾ cup cold water
½ cup milk
3 ¼ cups baker's flour
1 ½ tbsps whole milk powder
2 tsp salt
⅓ cup sugar
1 tsp fresh yeast
2 tbsps butter

Butter Sheet

2 cups butter, room temperature

DIRECTIONS

Day 1: Make the Dough

1 In the bowl of your mixer, add the yeast, then the wet ingredients followed by the dry ingredients and butter.

2 Using the dough hook, mix on 1st speed for 4 minutes, then increase to 2nd speed and mix for another 2 minutes.

3 Remove your dough from the bowl and shape into a ball. Return your dough to the bowl, cover and let proof for 1.5 hours (until almost double in size) Then place it in the refrigerator to rest overnight.

Day 2: Butter Sheet

1 On a parchment lined baking sheet, flatten your butter and shape into a 6" square.

2 Refrigerate until firm, but still malleable. Check readiness by pressing it with your finger. If it doesn't move, it's too cold. If your finger goes through it, it's too warm. You should see a slight indent in the butter when pressed.

3 Remove your dough (from Day 1) from the refrigerator and place it on a floured surface. Gently press the dough to flatten to remove the air.

4 Using a rolling pin, roll your dough into a 10" square, it should be about ½" thick.

5 Place the butter so that it is diamond shaped on top of the dough.

6 Pull and fold the dough corners into the center of the butter, using opposite corners to create an envelope (see image for reference, page 158). The butter should be completely covered by the dough and not exposed.

7 Starting from the center, tap your dough firmly using your rolling pin. Press the dough from the center outward. When you get to the end, return to the center, and repeat in the opposite direction. This will adhere the dough to the butter. This is also the beginning of elongating the dough. *You should not be rolling out the dough at this point, just pressing it as it stretches.*

8 Begin rolling your dough starting in the middle so you are encouraging the dough to elongate. Continue rolling until your dough is 24" long. If the dough is tight and wants to shrink, stop, and let the dough relax for 1 minute.

9 Note: You must repeat steps 9, 10, & 11 three times. Fold your dough into thirds by taking a third of the dough and pulling it towards the center. It's very important to make sure that the edge of the dough is straight, gently stretch it as necessary. Fold over the other side of the dough to the center, make sure that edge is straight, and the corners are squared. It should be roughly an 8" square. This is how you create the buttery layers of your croissant.

10 Wrap the dough with saran wrap to ensure that it does not dry out and place in the fridge for at least 30 minutes. You want to make sure the dough has time to relax and chill, a cold dough is easier to work with.

11 Take your dough out of the fridge and place it on the open side; the top flap (side) is facing toward you. Now rotate the dough one quarter, turn to the right (this will help you to roll in the opposite direction each time). Use your rolling pin to tap the dough and stretch it out, and finally roll the dough forward and backward until it is 24" long.

12 Once you have completed 3 folds. Place your dough in the refrigerator to chill for 30 minutes.

13 Remove the dough from the refrigerator. Measure the dough, with the top open part facing you. It should be 7-7.5" wide, if it's not, press and roll the dough until it is.

14 Roll the dough until it is 36-38" long and only ¼" thick. *If it shrinks, let it rest 1 minute, then try again.*

15 Cut your length of dough into isosceles triangles. You will trim the left edge off so that it is diagonal. The base of the triangle will measure about 4.5" long. Cut the other side of the triangle so it meets the tip.

16 Roll the piece starting from the base of the triangle and roll towards the tip, keeping the dough tight and widening your hands as you roll.

17 Place your croissant onto a parchment lined baking sheet. Curve the sides of your croissants so they form a "C" shape. Keep a 3" space between each. Then let them chill in the refrigerator overnight.

Day 3: Finish & Bake

1 Remove from the refrigerator and place your tray in a warm area of your kitchen such as on top of your fridge or a sunny spot on your counter. Let your croissants rise until they double in size (at least 2 hours). *When it's properly proofed, they should feel marshmallowy to the touch and the layers will be more visible.*

2 Mix one egg with a little water and gently brush over the top of your croissants.

3 Preheat your oven to 400°F.

4 Place your croissants in the oven at 400°F for 6 minutes. Without opening the door, reduce the temperature to 350°F and continue baking for another 15 minutes. Rotate the tray halfway through the bake.

Technique Images on page 158

CHOCOLATE CROISSANTS

3 DAY PROCESS | This is a variation of the *Butter Croissants* recipe, page 154.

INGREDIENTS

In addition to the ingredients for *Butter Croissants*:

Chocolate Sticks

Variation: Chocolate Croissant

Follow all the previous butter croissants steps until the end of step 14, then continue with these directions:

1 Cut the rolled-out dough 3.5" long rectangles.

2 Place your chocolate sticks at the bottom of the dough, and one around the middle of the dough. Roll the dough starting at the bottom, keeping it tight.

3 Place your chocolate croissants onto a parchment lined baking sheet, seam side down, keep 3-inch space between pieces. Let your chocolate croissants chill in the refrigerator overnight.

4 To bake, follow the Day 3 Butter Croissants instructions, page 154.

CROISSANT FOLDING TECHNIQUE

Steps 4-9 in recipe

01

02

05

06

Croissant-making is an intricate dance of dough and butter, where precise folds are key to achieving those flaky, buttery layers. The photos will walk you through each stage, from the initial roll-out to the final fold.

Butter Croissant recipe, page 154
Chocolate Croissant recipe, page 156

THE ART OF **PASTRY**

RASPBERRY SCONES

Yield: Makes 11 Scones

INGREDIENTS

2 ½ cups all-purpose flour
¾ cup pastry flour
½ cup white sugar
1 ½ tbsps baking powder
2 ½ cups cream (35%)
1 tsp vanilla extract
1 cup frozen raspberries

DIRECTIONS

1 Preheat your oven to 325°F.

2 In the bowl of your stand mixer pour in the cream, followed by all the ingredients except the raspberries.

3 Mix on first speed until the flour is mostly incorporated.

4 Add in the raspberry and mix until just combined. Careful not to over mix, we want to see pieces of raspberries not a pink mixture.

5 Using a parchment lined oven tray that fits in your freezer, shape your mixture into an 8" round. You can do this on a lightly floured surface to help with working your dough as it will be slightly wet.

6 Freeze until firm but still able to be cut.

7 Cut into 10 wedges and put back into your freezer until they are solid.

8 Separate the wedges and place on a parchment baking sheet about 2" apart. Top with granulated sugar for a tasty crust.

9 Bake at 325°F for 25 minutes.

CHEDDAR & CHIVE SCONES

Yield: Makes 10 Scones

INGREDIENTS

½ tbsp onion powder
2 whole eggs
1 cup + 2 tbsp cream (35%)
1 ½ cups cheddar cheese, shredded
2 tbsps sliced chives
3 ½ cups all-purpose flour
½ cup granulated sugar
⅛ cup baking powder
⅓ cup cubed butter

DIRECTIONS

1 Cut your butter into small pieces and place in fridge.

2 Once the butter is cold, place all the ingredients in the mixer bowl with the paddle attachment. Mix on low speed until fully incorporated. Scrape down the paddle occasionally to ensure all the butter is being incorporated. No pieces of butter should be visible, and the mixture should be fluffy.

3 Put the dry scone mixture in the fridge. Keeps for up to 1 month.

4 Preheat oven to 375°F.

5 In the bowl of a stand mixer, pour in the cream and whole eggs, then mix until fully combined.

6 Add the remaining ingredients, including the dry scone mix, to the milk and eggs. Mix on low speed until fully combined.

7 Scrape the scone mix onto your counter and shape it into a disc.

8 Roll the mix with a rolling pin until it is 1" thick. Using a 3" cookie cutter cut as many circles as possible.

9 Being careful not to over mix, combine your leftover dough and reshape into a disc. Reroll and cut the rest.

10 Place your scones on a parchment lined baking tray so they are 2" apart.

11 Top with extra cheese and bake for 25 minutes.

12 They should be golden brown on top and no crumbs when tested with a knife. Cool on the tray.

PÂTE SUCRÉE (TART SHELLS)

Yield: Makes 24 x 3" Diameter Tarts

These can be used for *Lemon Tarts* page 164 or *Banana Tarts* page 165.

INGREDIENTS

2 ½ cups butter
1 ½ cups granulated sugar
1 ¼ cups almond flour
1 tsp salt
4 ¼ cups pastry flour
2 whole eggs

DIRECTIONS

1 In a mixing bowl, add the sugar, almond flour and butter. Use a paddle attachment and mix until just combined.

2 Scrape the bottom of the bowl. Add the eggs and mix.

3 Add the pastry flour and mix.

4 Remove from the bowl and form into a ball. Wrap and put in fridge for 1 hour.

5 Preheat the oven to 350°F.

6 Roll to 0.4" thickness and cut circles about an inch larger than your tart shells and place them on a parchment lined tray. Use a fork to lightly punch holes in the dough to prevent air bubbles in the tart dough.

7 Refrigerate tart shells for 10 minutes. *The key is to keep the dough cool at all times.*

8 Spray the tart molds with nonstick spray and shape the tarts. Press into the edges and trim the top.

9 Par bake the tarts for 10 minutes.

LEMON TARTS

Yield: Makes 12 x 3" Diameter Tarts

INGREDIENTS

juice + zest of 1 lemon
⅓ cup granulated sugar
1 whole egg
⅛ cup cornstarch
⅔ cup melted butter
10 whole eggs
3 ¼ cups granulated sugar
1 tbsp lemon juice
3 tbsps cornstarch
2 cups butter
Par-baked *Pâte Sucrée Tart Shells*, page 163

Baking Note:

When melting the butter ensure it isn't too hot, but warm. If the butter is too hot it will cook the eggs.

DIRECTIONS

Fruit Paste

1 Mix the sugar and cornstarch together.

2 Add juice, zest and eggs.

3 Add in the melted butter just before it is ready to pour into the shells.

Lemon Curd

1 In a large bowl mix the sugar and cornstarch together.

2 Add the lemon juice and eggs and mix well.

3 Using a bain-marie, cook the mixture on medium heat, stirring often and scrape down the sides of the pot until the curd is thick.

4 Lastly, add the butter and mix well.

Assembly & Baking

1 Preheat the oven to 375°F.

2 Add a thin layer of fruit paste (approximately 2 tbsp) into the previously par baked *Pâte Sucrée* tart base shells, recipe on page 163.

3 Bake for 10-12 minutes. Make sure the crust is golden and the paste is set but not brown.

4 Pour the lemon curd over the fruit paste to the top of the tart shell and chill until set. Approximately 60 minutes.

Optional for presentation: Sprinkle the top with granulated sugar and torch until golden brown.

BANANA TARTS

Yield: Makes 24 x 3" Diameter Tarts

INGREDIENTS

7 whole eggs
1 ½ cups melted butter
1 ¼ cups granulated sugar
1 banana, sliced
a splash rum (optional)
Pâte Sucrée Tart Shells, page 163
Cream Topping, page 166

Baking Note:

Tart filling cannot be made in advance. Must be used immediately.

DIRECTIONS

1 Preheat the oven to 375°F.

2 Combine the eggs and sugar and mix well.

3 Slowly add in the melted butter until it is fully incorporated. It's important to make sure that the butter does not get cold and lumpy.

4 Spray the tart molds with nonstick spray. To ensure your tarts are removed without breaking, line your tart molds with a strip of parchment before pressing the dough into the edges of the mold.

5 Fill your par-baked *Pâte Sucrée* tart shells with thinly sliced bananas all the way to the top of the shell. You will think it's too much, but it's not, they will reduce as they cook.

6 Pour the tart filling mix on top to fill the tart. Make sure the mix does not go between the shell and the dough.

7 Bake at 375°F for 30 minutes.

8 Let the tarts cool down in the fridge then unmold.

9 Fill a pastry bag with your *Cream Topping* page 166, and decorate the tops of your banana tarts.

10 Chill for at least 20 minutes before serving.

Optional for presentation: Right away out of the oven, pour some liquid rum on top of each tart and torch until golden brown.

CREAM TOPPING

Can be used for *Banana Tarts*, recipe on page 165

INGREDIENTS

1 cup *Vanilla Pastry Cream*, page 173
¼ cup whipped cream
1 tsp rum

DIRECTIONS

1 Whip the whipping cream until firm and keep ¼ cup. (You can use the rest in your hot chocolate)

2 Whisk the pastry cream until smooth and fold it into the whipped cream along with the rum.

3 Fill a pastry bag with your cream topping and decorate the tops of your banana tarts.

4 Chill for at least 20 minutes before serving.

ART IS IN
HOT CHOCOLATE

Yield: Serves 3-4 People

INGREDIENTS

2 cups chocolate (64%)
1 cup whole milk powder
1 tsp cornstarch
⅓ cup milk
3 cups water

DIRECTIONS

1. On a cutting board, chop your chocolate into small pieces.
2. Mix all your ingredients together in a saucepan.
3. Bring to a boil stirring often to avoid burning the bottom.
4. Once it becomes thicker, it is ready to serve and enjoy!

OLD-FASHIONED POTATO BUTTERMILK DONUTS

Yield: Makes 9 Donuts

INGREDIENTS

¾ cup potato purée
2 cups buttermilk
2 whole eggs
1 tsp vanilla extract
1 cup + 1 tbsp sugar
1 tsp salt
5 cups all-purpose flour
¾ cup shortening
3 tbsps yeast

DIRECTIONS

1 Place the liquid ingredients in the bottom of a mixing bowl along with the yeast.

2 Add the potato purée and the dry ingredients, then finish by adding the shortening on top.

3 Mix using the dough hook attachment for 4 minutes, then increase the speed to medium-low and mix for another 4 minutes until the dough becomes elastic. It should start coming off the sides of the bowl and form into a ball shape.

4 Place your dough on a floured surface and shape it into a tight ball. Transfer it to an oiled medium-sized bowl and cover with plastic wrap. Let it sit at room temperature for 30 minutes, or until it doubles in size.

5 Place oil into a medium-sized pot, filling it about halfway, enough for the donuts to float while cooking. Turn the heat to medium and heat the oil to 350°F, using a thermometer to monitor the temperature.

6 Transfer the dough to a floured surface. Press the dough ball to remove any air, then roll it out to a 2-inch thickness then let the dough relax for 2 minutes.

7 Cut the donuts using a 3-inch circle cutter, then cut a hole from the middle. Place the dough on a parchment-lined baking sheet and let it proof until it doubles in size.

8 Fry at 350°F until golden brown on each side, around 4 minutes per side. Remove from the oil and let drain on a wire rack.

9 Dip in maple glaze while they are still hot.

Maple Glaze

¾ cup milk
¼ cup butter
1 cup maple syrup
1 tbsp vanilla extract
4 cups icing sugar

1 Heat milk, butter, and vanilla together until it comes to a boil.

2 Add the icing sugar in a mixing bowl with paddle attachment.

3 Add in the heated wet ingredients and mix until combined.

4 Add the maple syrup.

5 Strain glaze to remove any lumps.

Storage: The glaze can be kept in your fridge up to 1 month.

BERLINERS

Yield: Makes 15 Berliners

Berliners are delicious on their own, but they can also be tossed in cinnamon sugar directly after frying. We also like to stuff them with our *Raspberry Jam* page 172, *Chocolate Crémeux* page 151, *Vanilla Pastry Cream* page 173, or anything your taste buds can think of!

INGREDIENTS

Starter
1 ½ cups all-purpose flour
¾ cup water
1 tsp fresh yeast

Dough
1 ½ cups all-purpose flour
2 tsp salt
¼ cup sugar
4 egg yolks
5 tsp fresh yeast
¼ cup milk
¼ cup + 1 tbsp butter

Tools
Piping Bag & Piping Tip
Pairng Knife

DIRECTIONS

1 Mix your starter ingredients until combined. Cover and leave out up to 4 hours at room temperature. It should start to create bubbles and have a fermentation smell.

2 In a separate mixer bowl, add milk, butter, egg yolks and yeast.

3 Mix for 4 minutes on low speed, then for 10-15 minutes on medium-low speed. The dough should become shiny and elastic.

4 Mix for 4 minutes on 1st speed, then for 10-15 minutes on 2nd speed. You want your dough to be shiny and elastic.

5 Divide your dough into 15 pieces and shape them into balls. Place them on a parchment-lined baking tray covered with a tea towel and leave to proof at room temperature in a warmer area for 1 hour or until they double in size.

6 In a medium saucepan, heat oil over medium heat to reach 350°F.

7 Once your oil has reached temperature and your dough has doubled in size, you can fry your berliners. About 3 minutes per side.

8 Once fried, transfer the berliners onto a baking sheet with a tea towel to absorb the extra oil.

FILLING YOUR BERLINERS

Prepare the Piping Bag
Fill a piping bag with your desired filling, ensuring it is securely sealed to prevent leaks. Attach an appropriate piping tip for easy filling.

Prepare the Berliner
Use a paring knife to carefully make a small hole on the side of the Berliner, ensuring it's just large enough for the piping tip.

Fill the Berliner
Insert the piping tip into the hole, being careful not to push through the other side. Gently squeeze the bag to fill the Berliner with your desired amount of filling. Avoid overfilling to prevent the filling from bursting out.

RASPBERRY JAM

Yield: Makes 1 ½ to 2 cups of Jam

This recipe works best with frozen raspberries. Other frozen fruits may have more or less water, which could change the results of your jam.

INGREDIENTS

4 ½ **cups frozen raspberries**
1 ¼ **cups granulated sugar**
¼ **cup lemon juice**

DIRECTIONS

1 In a medium saucepan, thaw out the raspberries over medium heat. As they defrost, stir them often, by doing so, you will also break down the fruit which is what we are looking for.

2 Once they have thawed, add sugar, and bring to a boil.

3 Reduce heat to low and simmer for 15-20 minutes while stirring often to avoid sticking at the bottom of the pan. You will know your jam is ready once the white foam on the top disappears.

4 To check the thickness, grab two spoons. Dip one into the jam and take the handle of the other one and swipe through the jam on the back of the spoon. If the jam doesn't drip down into the stream, it is thick enough. If it drips, keep cooking it.

5 Once you've achieved the desired consistency, take your jam off the stove, and add the lemon juice. Mix well, and let cool.

Storage: The jam can be kept in an airtight container in the fridge for up to 1 month.

VANILLA PASTRY CREAM

This can be used to fill the *Macarons*, page 146.

INGREDIENTS

1 cup milk
1 tsp vanilla extract
¼ cup granulated sugar
⅛ cup cornstarch
4 egg yolks
1 tbsp butter

DIRECTIONS

1 Wrap a baking tray or plate in saran wrap and set aside.

2 Add milk and vanilla extract to a saucepan and bring to a boil over medium heat. *Be careful not to burn your milk.*

3 In a bowl, whisk sugar and corn starch together.

4 Add your eggs to the sugar and cornstarch.

5 Temper milk into egg, by slowly adding ⅓ of the heated milk to sugar and cornstarch mixture.

6 Pour your tempered mixture into the saucepan with the warm milk over medium heat.

7 Continue whisking vigorously and scraping with spatula until it comes to a boil.

8 Take off heat and add butter and whisk until incorporated.

9 Pour onto wrapped tray and cover with plastic wrap. Chill in the refrigerator for at least 60 minutes. Once chilled, scrape your pastry cream off the plastic wrap, and it's ready to use.

Storage: The pastry cream can be stored in an airtight container for up to 3 days.

CANELÉS DE BORDEAUX

Yield: Makes 18 canelés

This recipe was tested in a traditional copper canelé mold. It can also be made in small muffin tins, but cooking time may vary.

INGREDIENTS

2 cups milk

1 tsp vanilla extract

2 whole eggs

2 egg yolks

1 ¼ cups granulated sugar

¾ cup all-purpose flour

¼ cup melted butter

¼ cup rum

DIRECTIONS

1 Preheat your oven to 400°F.

2 Place your milk, vanilla and butter in a saucepan and warm over medium heat until it reaches 60°C.

3 Mix sugar and flour together.

4 Mix the eggs, yolks, and rum together, then add warm milk to the egg mixture.

5 Fold the liquid mixture into your dry mix until well incorporated. Your batter will have the consistency of cream. Let your batter rest in the fridge for at least 60 minutes. *This is very important as your batter must be cold when it is poured into the hot mold.*

6 Place your canelé molds on a tray and into the oven for at least 15 minutes. *Your molds must be piping hot when you pour your cold batter into them.*

7 Remove your molds from the oven and spray with avocado oil spray. Pour the cold batter into the hot mold until it barely reaches the rim.

8 Bake at 400°F for 20 minutes, then turn your oven down to 350°F and cook for another 60 minutes.

9 Once they are cooked, remove the canelés from the oven and pop them out of the molds immediately.

PÂTE BRISÉE

Yield: Makes 1 Dough Ball, enough for one pie shell

INGREDIENTS

1 whole egg
1 cup diced butter (cold)
½ cup water
1 tsp salt
3 ½ cups all-purpose flour

DIRECTIONS

1 In a stand-up mixer with the paddle attachment put the flour, salt and cold butter cubes and mix.

2 Scrape the bottom of the bowl and the paddle to ensure that the butter is properly mixing in.

3 Careful not to overmix, you are looking for the butter to be fully incorporated and the mix to be fluffy.

4 In a separate bowl, mix the water and egg together.

5 Slowly add the liquid mixture to your dry ingredients.

6 Once your dough has taken shape, put it on a lightly floured surface and work it into a ball.

7 Cover your dough ball and let it rest in the fridge.

Storage: This pâte brisée dough can be kept up to 5 days in the fridge, and 1 month in the freezer!

PUFF PASTRY

This *Puff Pastry* can be used for any recipe that calls for it.

INGREDIENTS

Part A
2 cups diced butter, room temp
¼ cup all-purpose flour

Part B
¾ cup pastry flour
1 ¾ cups all-purpose flour
1 tbsp salt
¼ cup butter, melted (but not hot)
¾ cup room temp water

DIRECTIONS

1 Place your ingredients of Part A together and mix on low speed using a paddle attachment until just combined.

2 Lay your butter and flour mix (Part A) on parchment-lined baking sheet and shape it into a 7"x12" rectangle using a spatula. It should be about 1/4" thick. Chill in the refrigerator until firm, but not solid.

3 Add the dry ingredients into your mixing bowl and turn the mixer onto low speed while slowly adding the melted butter.

4 Once butter is incorporated, slowly add your water until your dough comes together. Cover your dough with a cloth and let it rest for 10 minutes.

5 Lay your dough (Part B) on a parchment-lined baking sheet and shape it into a 7x5" rectangle using a spatula. It should be 1/4" thick. You want the length of your dough to match the width of your chilled butter (Part A).

6 Chill the dough for 20 minutes.

7 Once chilled, place the butter on your surface and place the dough in the centre so that the dough and the butter are lined up on the top and bottom and there is a 3.5" flap of butter on both sides.

8 Fold the butter flaps around the dough, making sure that the sides match up and no dough is peaking through.

9 Starting at the centre of your dough and butter bundle, use your rolling pin to tap out towards the ends to elongate the dough before rolling.

10 Roll out until you reach 18-24" long.

11 Now make a double "book fold" over one edge of the dough until it is folded over 1/4 of the head of the dough. Fold over the other edge and line it up with the other side. The edges should meet but not overlap.

12 Pull the dough gently to adjust the sides. Fold that dough in half so that the edges are in the middle of the head.

13 Saran wrap and chill in the fridge for 1 hour.

14 Remove form the saran wrap and repeat the process of rolling out to 18-24" and make a double fold, two more times. Make sure to chill the dough for one hour in between folds.

15 You now have Puff Pastry dough ready to use for any recipe.

GALETTE DES ROIS

Yield: Serves 6-8 People | This recipe is made using the *Puff Pastry* page 178.

INGREDIENTS

Part A: Puff Pastry Discs

Puff Pastry, page 178

DIRECTIONS

1 Make the *Gallette des Rois* using the *Puff Pastry* recipe, page 178, which has rested overnight in the fridge.

2 Lay your dough on a lightly floured surface and let it rest for 2 minutes. Loosen the dough from the surface and allow it to relax, untacked.

3 Cut your dough into two 8" rounds. You can use a ring cutter if you have one or you can use an 8" pie pan as a guide to cut out the shape using a sharp knife.

4 Your cut rounds can be wrapped in plastic and refrigerated. *The less you touch the puff, the nicer it will rise.*

Part B: Galette Cream

- 1 cup *Pastry Cream,* page 173
- 1 cup butter
- 1 cup ground almonds
- ¾ cup icing sugar
- 1 tbsp cornstarch
- 2 eggs, room temp
- 1 tbsp pistachio paste

1 Mix your pastry cream and pistachio paste together until smooth. Set aside.

2 In a separate bowl, whip the butter, sugar, cornstarch, and ground almonds together until fluffy.

3 Once the mixture is fluffy, add the eggs and mix.

4 Add the pistachio and pastry cream mixture to the bowl and mix with a paddle until smooth.

Storage: Your pistachio cream can be stored in the fridge overnight or used right away.

Part C: Assemble

Egg wash
Puff discs
¼ cup of honey
1 tsp of water

Tools

Soft brush
Paring knife
Piping bag
A small piping tip
Baking trays
Parchment paper

Optional

Small jewel or figurine (after the cake is cut, whoever gets the jewel wins a prize)

1 Place the puff discs on a lightly flour-dusted surface and brush egg wash carefully around the edge to about 1.5".

2 Fill your piping bag with your Pistachio Cream, starting in the centre and working your way to no more than 1" from the outside.

3 Place one jewel on cream and cover your galette with the second puff pastry disc.

4 Gently press the edges together to seal the galette. Make sure its sealed very well. If it's not sticking together, use a bit more egg wash until it sticks.

5 Once the galette is sealed, carefully flip it over and place it flat-side up on a parchment-lined baking tray.

6 Egg wash with a soft brush once and refrigerate.

7 Once your egg wash is dry, you can use the back end of the pairing knife to score a design on top of your galette and poke 4-6 holes to let the steam escape. Then, egg wash one more time and refrigerate for one hour.

8 Pre-heat your oven at 350°.

9 Make a honey glaze by mixing ¼ cup of honey with 1 tsp of water.

10 After 1 hour, place your cold galette into the hot oven and bake for 45 minutes, or until the top is caramelized and shiny.

11 As soon as it is out of the oven, gently brush the hot galette with the honey glaze to give a beautiful shine. Let cool for 20 minutes before cutting and serving.

In Loving Memory of
Kevin Mathieson

In the vibrant tapestry of New York City's culinary scene, Kevin Mathieson emerged not only as an exceptional chef but also as a beloved friend and true artist. As the visionary force behind the culinary magic at Payard, Kevin's dedication and passion for his craft were unparalleled. This cookbook is not just a collection of recipes; it is a tribute to a beautiful soul whose culinary journey was marked by love, innovation, and an unyielding commitment to excellence.

Kevin was more than a chef; he was a mentor, a pioneer, and an inspiration to all fortunate enough to cross paths with him. From his early days at Payard, to becoming a celebrated culinary artist, Kevin's impact on the food industry was profound. His ability to push the limits of creativity, coupled with a genuine and kind spirit, made him a cherished mentor to many.

In these pages, you will find the essence of Kevin's culinary genius—a celebration of flavors, techniques, and the unbridled joy he brought to the kitchen. Through his expertise, he not only elevated the dining experience at Payard but left an indelible mark on countless aspiring chefs.

This cookbook serves as a testament to his legacy, a legacy that goes beyond the confines of the kitchen and into the hearts of those who knew him. Kevin Mathieson flourished not only in his professional life, but also as a devoted husband and father.

As we navigate the recipes within, let us remember the man behind the flavors—a trailblazer whose love for his craft was surpassed only by his love for family and friends. Though Kevin may no longer be with us, his spirit lives on in every dish and in the cherished memories of those lucky enough to have been touched by his warmth and talent.

I am thankful for the privilege of having called Kevin Mathieson a friend and colleague, proud of the moments we shared at Payard, and honored to present this cookbook in celebration of his extraordinary life and culinary legacy. May these recipes not only tantalize your taste buds but also serve as a reminder of the true artistry that Kevin brought to every plate. Cheers to a culinary maestro, a pioneer, and a friend whose impact will forever be etched in the history of our kitchen and our hearts.

François Payard
Chef and Mentor, New York City

This cookbook is a tribute to my beloved husband Kevin whose passion for cooking and baking brought joy and flavour to our lives.

Every dish Kevin created was a masterpiece filled with creativity, care and the love he poured into every meal. I'll always remember how he turned family dinners into feasts, teaching our kids to cook with laughter and patience.

This collection of recipes is our way of sharing Kevin's culinary artistry with the world and ensuring his legacy continues to inspire others.

Kevin, it was your dream to put out a cookbook and I hope this brings that dream to life, honouring the love and inspiration you shared with all of us.

You remain forever in my heart.

Stephanie

From day one, Kevin knew exactly what he was doing...he tried to gain our love and our trust one chewy cookie; one blown sugar structure; one freshly baked dynamite at a time. And it worked. Kevin took us in as his own, he had a heart of gold and the spirit of a child. The smell of caramelized onions, rosemary and yeast will always remain comforting to us as he would come home, a box of fresh croissants in hand, from a full night of baking, making sure every time to have energy left to run around the house with us. Spontaneous weekend trips, food fights, foie gras stuffed chicken, crazy Thai dinners...never a dull moment since he came into our lives. He brought the inner child out of us & taught us not to take life too seriously. Sharing his passion of food through a recipe book was always a dream of his, we hope his food brings you joy the same way it did for us growing up.

With Love,

Emma & Mayou
Stepdaughters

The Mathieson Family

My brother Kevin was a humble, kind, generous and loving man. I have always been so proud of his accomplishments and successes in life. As a child, we would have a big family breakfast every weekend, one would make the toast, one would cook the bacon and the other one would make the eggs. Mom would always get us involved with cooking and baking. We would always make caramel popcorn every Friday and hang out. As we became older, I would come home to Kevin having dinner parties with his friends. He would cook a nice meal for them and mom would do all the dishes for him. We used to love going for brunch at the Fort Garry and seeing all the desserts that Kevin was making as a pastry chef on Sundays. I have a fond memory when he won 1st place at a cake decorating show at a hotel. We were all so proud of him. Kevin would always make delicious food. He could whip something up in minutes and it would always taste scrumptious; I would always have seconds.

Thanks Ti kev for all the memories, I love and miss you always and forever.

Lydia Mathieson
Sister

My dear friend, from day one you took me in and under your wing. My work ethic and standards for quality are because of you. You encouraged and inspired me to stay focused and hungry. To not be intimidated, but focus on progress. Kevin Mathieson you were the hardest working human I have ever met. You truly lived and were present where you stood; body, mind, heart and soul. You brought fire, real passion and an endless thirst as you pursued excellence. My first NY mate. I'll greatly miss troubleshooting recipes and sharing business notes. I'll always cherish our many calls, our trips together and damn, I'm so happy we drove that ferrari. Without a doubt I am most honored to have known you as a father, your legacy is the love you shared with your precious children. Thank you for everything you've done for me, and until we meet again, know I miss you my brother and
I will cherish our memories.

Marius Pop Ferrari
Portland, Oregon USA

Kevin - We were so young. It was 1998, almost the same age, and we both had our whole lives ahead of us. Different cultures and from two different countries - but one thing we had in common was a good laugh. I can say that this time in my life were some of my best years.

We were such a good team, and it was a pleasure working side by side. To this day, any time I think about our time in the kitchen, it brings a smile to my face. I was lucky to work with you, Kevin.

When you came to visit me at the Wynn Hotel with Stephanie, you told me about the business you built together, and I was so proud and happy for you. I shared that I also wanted to open my own business as well, and your advice was so helpful. And when I did open, you found a way to come and check on me with Stephanie and Marius.

You were someone who cared for the quality of the job you did, but most importantly the people you love.

Pierre Gatel
Las Vegas, USA

I remember you the day we met: you had come from far away, from Canada, I had also come from far away, from France, we had just been parachuted into New York. I was full of my "French-style" certainties, you were full of questions, ambition and curiosity. You wanted to know, discover and understand everything about this business. What a pleasure it was to work with you, I remember your laughter that spread through the lab and lit us all up. We saw little of each other, but like true friends, the only ones who count, a phone call, a message and we were ready for each other as if we were still in New York. Not a day goes by that I don't think of you. You're my friend.

Nicolas Berger
Paris, France

He was the Miles Davis of the food world. A true artist that could make something extremely special with a simple ingredient. He spread love everywhere he went, and I feel so privileged to have called him my best friend. My dear Kevin, you are missed. I love you forever brother.

Steph Lariviere
Gatineau, QC

Big K,

Your passion for food was magnetic—so much so that it was sometimes misunderstood. When life got tough, whether it was the ups and downs of business, the struggles of the pandemic, or moments of ill health, you always found your way back to the kitchen. It was your sanctuary, the place where you could create and share your incredible gift with the people you loved.

I'm so glad I have so many memories of you cooking up feasts, along with photos of you completely in your element, manifesting your passion and creativity through every dish.

Your legacy lives on, not only in the recipes you created but in the care and thoughtfulness you poured into every family meal and every Art Is In bakery special that Emma insisted I try.

You'll always be in our hearts... and of course, in our stomachs too.

Farid Dagher
Friend & Son-in-law

Kevin and I go back, way back, to toddler age in fact. In a way food saved my life, more specifically hospitality as a profession. I have Kevin to thank for that. He helped me find my path in this crazy business and also helped me develop a deeper understanding of food and cooking which lead to a lifestyle but more importantly to a commitment. Without commitment and passion there is no life or reward in the restaurant business.

Kevin lived and breathed food. It's extremely rare to find a master of pastry and savory cuisine. From the age of 12 all he spoke about was becoming a chef. He practiced at home in the kitchen using his mom's garden fresh produce, then studied culinary arts in middle school up to high school. Professional kitchens became his life and he traveled the world in search of knowledge.

Art~is~in was so personal to Kevin because he created it from his memories and experiences. Its food was his story. He was passionate and uncompromising in his vision and that's why it exists without him and through all of the friends, family, and colleagues involved. He created a village and a culture to carry his food story forward into the future to share with the world.

All of us can still taste Kevin's love through the passion he poured into this Ottawa institution. He lives on like the fermented live yeast strain "mother" he created and cared for lovingly keeping alive for years giving "birth" each day to more loaves of dynamite bread carrying forward this legacy.

This book is a true testament to Kevin's love, commitment, and passion for comfort food. All of us that knew Kevin have hearts that are so full with the thought of fulfilling this dream of Kevin's to share with the world.

With Love, Misses & Kisses,
Devin & Christine Nelles
Grenada

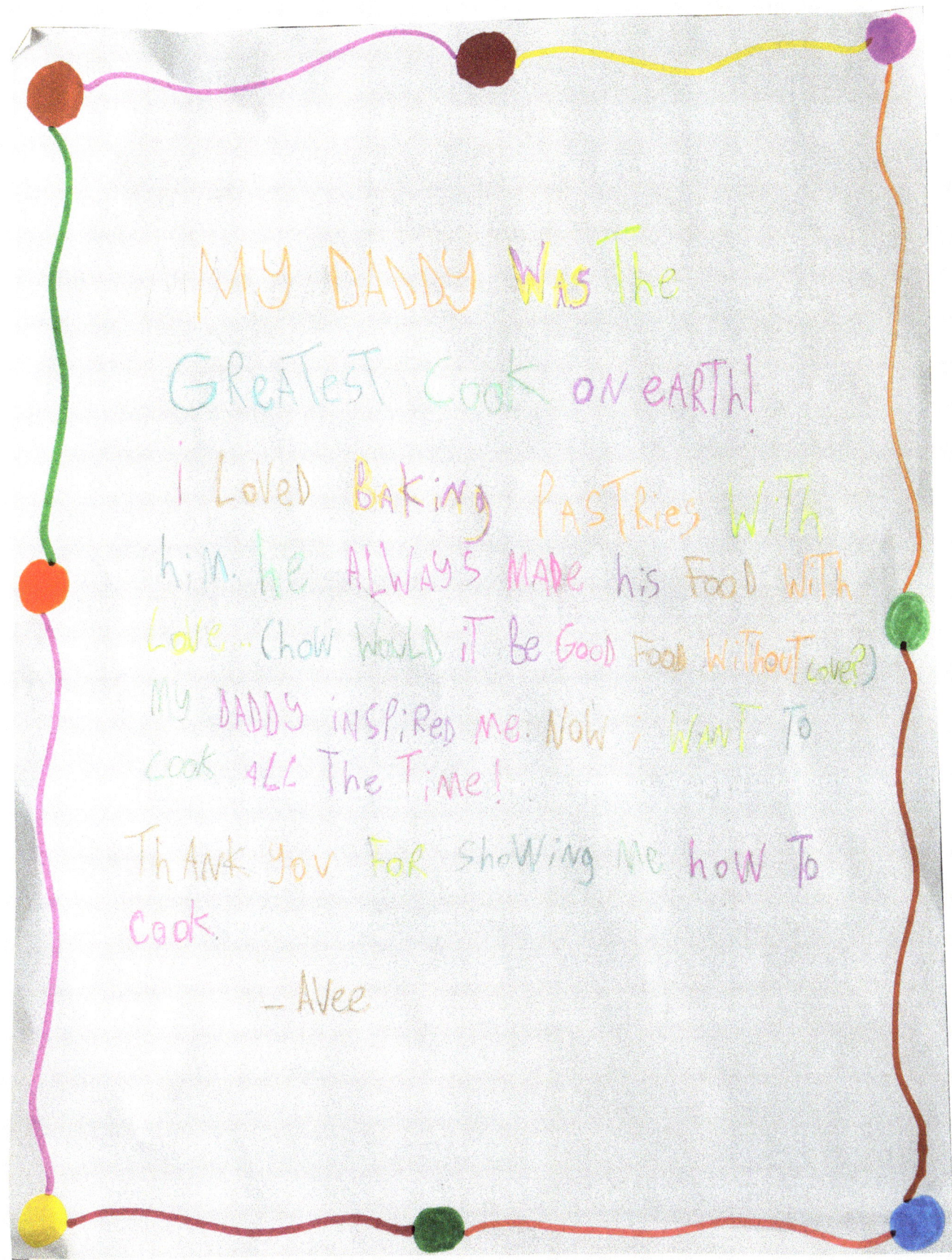

Avee, Age 10

Art Is In Bakery

250 City Centre Avenue, Unit #112
Ottawa, Ontario

www.ingramcontent.com/pod-product-compliance
Lightning Source LLC
LaVergne TN
LVHW072012060526
838200LV00011B/339